Anonymus

A thrilling personal Experience

Brooklyn's Horror

Anonymus

A thrilling personal Experience
Brooklyn's Horror

ISBN/EAN: 9783743345805

Manufactured in Europe, USA, Canada, Australia, Japa

Cover: Foto ©ninafisch / pixelio.de

Manufactured and distributed by brebook publishing software
(www.brebook.com)

Anonymus

A thrilling personal Experience

A

THRILLING PERSONAL EXPERIENCE!

BROOKLYN'S HORROR.

WHOLESALE HOLOCAUST AT THE BROOKLYN, NEW YORK, THEATRE,

ON THE

NIGHT OF DECEMBER 5TH, 1876.

Three Hundred Men, Women and Children
BURIED IN THE BLAZING RUINS!

ORIGIN, PROGRESS AND DEVASTATION OF THE FIRE.

The Tragedy in the Galleries — A Wedge of Death — Into a Pit of Fire —
Harrowing Scenes and Incidents — Affecting and Exciting Stones of
Survivors — Two Actors among the Victims — The Ghastly
Array of the Disfigured Dead — Heartrending Scenes
in Identifying the Remains — Complete List of
the Victims — Burial of the Dead.

PHILADELPHIA:
BARCLAY & CO., PUBLISHERS,
No. 21 NORTH SEVENTH STREET.

BURNING OF THE BROOKLYN THEATRE.

T HE destruction of the Brooklyn Theatre, on the night of Tuesday, December the 5th, was the most terrible calamity of its kind that has occurred in this country. What was first deemed to be an ordinary fire, naturally involving serious financial loss to the owners, the lessees and the actors, was really a catastrophe of the most heartrending character, causing, as it did, the loss of upwards of three hundred lives. No theatre fire on this continent had so much horror lent to it. Even the most stony-hearted were touched by the awfulness of this great calamity.

Three hundred human beings of both sexes and of all ages were thrust into eternity through an agonizing and painful death. They were thus doomed at a moment of pleasure and mental excitement over the mimic troubles of the dramatic personages in a play possessing features that touched the hearts of those who followed the scenes on the stage. At a moment when every eye was fixed on the painted scene, and every ear strained on the utterances of the several characters, the dreadful cry of "Fire!" was raised, and, in a few moments after, the entire building was filled with flame and smoke, and hundreds of men, women and children were suffocated and burned to death, and their charred and disfigured remains buried beneath the ruins.

Such is the simple and terse record of this most dreadful occurrence, and these few sentences afford such outline and visible form to the picture that it scarcely needs the shocking details that necessarily follow to give it color and ghastliness. That so much horror should attend the burning of a theatre sent a thrill of pain through every heart in the land. The full scope of the calamity and the dreadful scenes attending it are depicted in the accounts that follow.

No more awful moment can be imagined than that when the fire was discovered. The full moon of the fatal evening had tempted upwards of twelve hundred people from their homes, and lighted them to the brilliant entrance of the theatre. The famous play of the "Two Orphans," with an excellent cast, mainly from the Union Square Theatre, of New York city, was the attraction, and had renewed its fascinations over a public long since familiar with its story. The audience was characteristically a Brooklyn gathering. Many well-known citizens were there: among them the family of Mr. Wil-

liam C. Kingsley, the Hon. Henry C. Murphy, Edgar Cullen and ladies, E.
B. Dickinson and ladies, and Henry Beam.   The following was the distribu-
tion of characters in the play, and, with the exception of Miss Morant, Miss
Vernon and one or two of the minor characters, all the members were in the
theatre at the outbreak of the fire:

Chevalier De Vaudry	Mr. C. R. Thorne.
Count de Linieres, Minister of Police	Mr. H. F. Daly.
Picard, Valet to the Chevalier	Mr. Claude Burroughs.
Jacques Frochard, an Outlaw	Mr. J. B. Studley.
Pierre Frochard, his Brother	Mr. H. S. Murdoch.
Marquis de Presles	Mr. J. G. Peakes.
Doctor of the Hospitals St. Louis and Salpetriere.	Mr. H. B. Phillips.
La Fleur	Mr. H. W. Montgomery.
Officer of the Guard	Mr. John Mathews.
Martin	Mr. L. Thompson.
De Mailly	Mr. J. Clements.
D'Estres	Mr. George Dalton.
Footman	Mr. E. Lamb.
Antoine	Mr. R. Struthers.
Louise, ⎰ The ⎱	Miss Kate Claxton.
Henriette, ⎱ Two Orphans. ⎰	Miss Maude Harrison.
La Frochard	Mrs. Farren.
Countess de Linieres	Miss Fanny Morant.
Sister Genevieve	Miss Ida Vernon.
Marianna, an Outcast	Miss Kate Girard.
Julie	Miss Ethel Allen.
Cora	Miss L. Cleves.
Sister Therese	Mrs. L. E. Seymour.

The play had proceeded to the last scene of the last act.   The curtain had
just been rung up, revealing a scene of exciting and pathetic interest to the
audience.   It was the interior of the hovel boat-house on the Seine.   The
blind *Louise* (Miss Claxton) lay on a bed of straw; *Mme. Frochard* (Mrs.
Farren) was scraping a carrot; the cripple was at his wheel, and *Jacques*
was about to emphasize his brutality with a threat.   As was natural from
her reclining position, which enabled her to see the flies, the first flame
caught the eye of Miss Claxton.   Mr. Murdoch (*Pierre*) was delivering his
speech when the two heard a whisper of " Fire " from behind the scenes, and,
looking up, saw flames issuing from the flies.   Mr. Murdoch stopped, but
Miss Claxton whispered to him, "Go on, they will put it out, there will be a
panic—go on," and he resumed.   So far the audience had not noticed anything out of the way, and the two played the scene through, Mrs. Farren
(*Frochard*) entering meanwhile.   The carpenters were all the while trying to
stop the progress of the flames, unnoticed by the house, and Miss Claxton
delivered her little speech to *Jacques:* " I forbid you to touch me," which
was greeted with applause.   Meanwhile the audience had begun to suspect
something, and with Miss Claxton's words, " I will beg no more," the actors
were forced to move from fear of falling timber, and the audience rose to
their feet.   Mrs. Farren and Mr. Murdoch stepped to the footlights and
waved to the people to resume their seats, while Mr. Studley and Miss Claxton went forward to do likewise.   Mr. Studley shouted: " Ladies and gentle-

men, there will be no more of the play, of course; you can all go out if you will only keep quiet." Miss Claxton, at the other end of the stage, begged the people to keep cool, adding: " We are between you and the flames."

By this time the fire (which seems to have originated by some of the " short drops" blowing against the " border lights" in the flies, and so communicating to the scenery) had made so much headway that the actors had to look out for themselves. They had held their ground as long as it was possible, and, seeing from the panic which started immediately in the gallery and spread all over the upper part of the house, that the worst had begun, they began their retreat, the ground floor being already almost cleared. Mr. Thorne had gone. Mr. Burroughs was up-stairs in his dressing-room, from which he escaped only to meet his death. Mr. Murdoch was never seen again. Miss Claxton and Miss Harrison rushed one way; Miss Girard and the minor people another.

The sight of fire seemed to paralyze every one for an instant, and just as they recovered sufficiently to act, Mr. Studley's sudden coming to the front of the stage and assuring them that there was no cause for alarm caused another pause of a second. It was for a second only. The blazing fragments began falling thick and fast, contradicting the actor's well-intentioned deception. The audience arose as by one impulse and made a rush for the doors. The entreaties of Miss Claxton and Mr. Murdoch were unheeded. The fierce struggle for life had begun.

The ushers for the most part preserved their presence of mind and endeavored to enforce order among the rushing crowd, as did also the police in attendance. Mr. Rochfert, the head usher, broke open a small door at the farther end of the vestibule and increased the facilities of exit into the open air, which regularly consisted of two doors five feet wide, opening upon Washington street. Mr. Rochfert also entered the auditorium and endeavored to quell the excitement, but without effect.

A fire alarm had been immediately sent from the First Precinct Station-House, which is located next the theatre, and a minute or two after a general alarm and also a call for the reserved force of all the precincts. But by the time the engines were in position and at work the fire was beyond control. The occupants of the orchestra chairs and parquet had had but little difficulty in making good their escape, but at least two-thirds and perhaps even a larger fraction of the audience were still in the dress-circle and gallery. The lowest estimate of the number in the gallery is that five or six hundred people were in that portion of the house, and from among these were most of the three hundred deaths. The exit from the first balcony was down a single flight of stairs in the rear of the vestibule. Down these stairs the people came in scores, leaping and jumping in wild confusion. The way out from the upper gallery was down a short flight of stairs starting from the south wall of the building, thence by a short turn down a long flight against the same wall to the level of the balcony, and from this floor down a cased flight into Washington street. The main floor and first balcony were soon emptied through their respective exits, but for the five or six hundred panic-stricken gallery spectators to pass safely through the tortuous passage described was next to an impossibility.

Every indication points to the belief that, suffocated by the smoke forced down like a wall from the roof, the mass of those in the upper gallery thronged about the entrance to the stairs and were either blocked there so as to make exit impossible, or were unable even to make the attempt to escape, and sank down, one upon the other, to fall in a mass into the horrible pit under the vestibule when the supports of the gallery were burned away. Those near the entrance of the stairs were, probably, the only ones who were able to escape from this terrible slaughter-pen. There was comparatively little outcry here, and this again would seem to indicate that suffocation had intervened to numb the sensibilities of the hundreds to whom death was to come by fire.

As soon as the flames reached the rear of the theatre, near the entrances, where the hundreds of people were contending wildly, the horror of the scene was increased tenfold. Some leaped madly from the gallery upon the orchestra chairs, and only a few were sufficiently self-possessed to lower themselves by the railings. One man escaped by the small window at the head of the gallery stairs, letting himself down upon the roof of the station-house. Another, who attempted the same escape, was suffocated or became insensible as he reached the window, and was seen sitting motionless there until swept away. A few lowered themselves from the second-story windows on the Flood's alley side. But the great mass stood helplessly blocked in. The smoke became unbearable, and the police and firemen who had been able to penetrate the crowd at all were obliged to retire. They seized as many of the paralyzed bodies as they could and dragged them into the street, passing on their way out over piles of insensible men and boys. Fifteen minutes after the fire broke out the interior of the theatre was wrapped in flames. Shortly after the roof fell in, and, at 11.45, a half an hour after the fire started, the broad east wall fell with a terrible crash. The few who had reached the first flight of stairs from the street were taken out and carried into the First Precinct Station-House. The crowd that had escaped from the theatre remained in the adjacent streets. Men without hats or coats, with clothing torn and faces bruised; women bonnetless and dishevelled, weeping convulsively— every face was a picture of woe and fright.

The crowd was quickly and largely augmented by the anxious throng of sight-seers, and to keep them within the proper limits required the efforts of nearly the entire reserved police force of the city. The Police Commissioners and Superintendent Campbell, and Inspector Waddy; the Chief of the Fire Department, Thomas F. Nevins, and Fire Marshal Keady, had been telegraphed for and came promptly to the scene of the conflagration, and did everything in their power to provide for the sufferers, for many had been brought out bruised and burned. The firemen had not fairly begun their labors before it became evident that it was impossible to save the theatre or any part of it; the entire attention of the force was therefore directed to the surrounding buildings, which meanwhile were seriously threatened. Several small buildings on the opposite side of Flood's alley were partially destroyed, and at one time the First Precinct Station-House was in imminent danger. The fire was, however, confined to the theatre by the united exertions of the entire fire department. The interior decorations of the theatre were of such light

CLAUDE BURROUGHS.

H. S. MURDOCH.

and inflammable material that the fire was quite beyond their control, so far as the theatre was concerned, and the roof being equally light and inflammable, it required constant exertion to keep the fire from spreading.

At about three o'clock in the morning the fire had been nearly extinguished, and the major part of the throng of sight-seers had gone to their homes, ignorant of the fatal consequences of the conflagration.

The flames had subsided sufficiently to permit the firemen to make an investigation near the main entrance of the theatre. Chief Nevins passed over the trembling floor of the hallway toward the inner doorway. Inside the doors the flooring had fallen in, leaving a deep pit of fire and flame, from which a dense smoke and steam ascended. Here a sickening spectacle met his horrified gaze. Close up to the flaming furnace, and clinging to the splintered verge of the demolished flooring, was the body of a woman. Her hands clasped the frame-work of the door in a desperate grasp. She had fought hard for life. Evidently she would have escaped had not the flooring given way beneath her. All the clothing was burnt off, and the features were so blackened that she was unrecognizable, and the body was removed to the Morgue.

At 4 o'clock in the morning the flames were put out, and the heap of debris was black and cold. From the vestibule platform the firemen saw a most horrible spectacle. The mound that had at first appeared to be simply a heap of ashes proved to be almost wholly composed of human bodies. Heads, arms, legs, shoulders, shoes, and here and there entire human remains protruded through the surface of the mound. Policemen and firemen hesitated for a moment before leaping down upon the sickening heap. An inclined plane of plain deal boards was hastily constructed to reach from the tender vestibule platform to the pit, and upon this a ladder was rested. Upon the ladder the men went to and fro. Upon the plane, coffins were hauled up and down. At first the firemen lifted the bodies from the debris, after having carefully dug around them and loosened them, and ten minutes was consumed in exhuming each body. But as it became apparent that there were scores and scores of human remains, and that a day, and perhaps a night, would end before the last corpse was taken out, less tender means were used in the operation, and the work assumed a more earnest and energetic character. Instead of five men, ten men set at work among the ruins, while on the vestibule platform a dozen sturdy firemen manned the short ropes by which the coffins, laden with human remains, were drawn up and dragged to the sidewalk. All the bodies were bent into horrid shapes, assumed in the struggles of death by suffocation and by burning. Nine out of ten of the corpses had an arm upraised and bent to shield the face. Something was missing from every one. This one lacked a head or a foot, this a nose, an ear, or a hand, another its fingers or the crown of the skull. Very many broken limbs and protruding bones were found, and there were gashes in the upturned faces or fractures in the smooth-burned skulls, so that each corpse as it was dragged into the light was a new revelation of ghastliness. A few lusty pulls disengaged each body. Two or three men seized its stiffened limbs and pressed them into a coffin, a pair of sharp-pointed tongs clutched the coffin, and the firemen overhead dragged it even with the street, where a cloth was thrown over the coffin, and it was dragged to the dead-wagons, which kept coming and going all day long.

Opera glasses, chains, studs, purses, and even watches were found under and on the bodies, and were thrown to one side upon a spread-out newspaper. Opposite the main entrance at the rear of the theatre other firemen and police officers delved in the ashes and brought forth corpse after corpse to be boxed and carried away to the Morgue, with the same rapidity as at the other door. At four o'clock, when a hundred and forty-seven bodies had been exhumed on the Washington street side, fifty-three had been carried from the alley-way in the rear. Moving among the firemen, either as spectators or supervisors of the ghastly work, were Chief Engineer Nevins, Police Commissioner Hurd, Fire Commissioner McLaughlin, Assistant Engineer Farley, and ex-Police Superintendent Folk.

Surrounding the ruins, in Washington, Johnson and Adams streets, were throngs of people who stood close together on the sidewalks and left only room enough for one vehicle at a time to traverse the roadways. The dead wagons continually passing and repassing, kept this passage way clear, and were themselves the objects of the most interest. During the entire day there were continual quarrels between the police officers and the over-curious people. Pickpockets—nearly all boys—were numerous, and were brought into the First Precinct station two at a time. In the station were coats, and hats, canes, shawls, bundles, valises filled with costumes, and numerous other articles taken from the ruins of the theatre.

When the first wagon, laden with the dead from the fire, halted in front of the Morgue, the gathering pressed forward and crushed its way between the wagon and the doorway. The police officers appealed to the people to be calm, and at length the bodies were taken into the building.

Daylight had not set in when the arrival of the dead bodies was announced. It was thought at first that the first was the remains of a young woman, but a vest displaying a watch and chain was revealed. About nine o'clock the second body, that of a young man whose hands were clasped, and who wore a plain silver ring and a gutta percha ring, was received. Nicholas Kieley's remains were next, and the Rev. Father Kieley, who wept as though his heart was broken, recognized his brother.

Upon the body of the fourth corpse was a gold open-faced watch, to which was attached a thin gold chain. On the back of the watch was the words, "A mother's gift." The fifth body was that of a stalwart man, whose hands were fixed over his face. Then there was a negro whose features were beyond recognition. Following was a body whose head had been nearly consumed, and next one whose arms had been burned away. On this man was a bright gold collar button. Then there were the remains of a young woman. The limbs were drawn up, the body was twisted, and the features could not be recognized.

The remains of a boy about fourteen years of age were next carried in. A man with a checked shirt was put at his side. The bodies of three young boys and three girls were next received. On one of the bodies was a hunting-case silver watch, 76,744, with a gold chain and a piece of the Hell Gate telegraphic wire as a charm. The timepiece was in good order and marked the correct time.

Before 3 o'clock seventy-eight bodies were strewn about in the Morgue, and a long line of men and women were constantly passing in and out of the building. Nearly every person had permits from the Coroner's office, and the women visitors were in the majority.

A most shameful and vulgar feature of the inroad upon the Morgue was the vast number of women who, through mere curiosity, insisted upon entering the building. Women who were naturally nervous and hysterical forced their way in and risked good clothing and head dress in their wild attempts to hover over the bodies. They began to sob and gesticulate long before they reached the hallway in which twenty-three blackened corpses were in line on the marble floor.

When the women reached this scene they shrieked as though bereft of all their kindred, but the majority of them were forced to admit that they knew no one among the dead. Occasionally some agonized mother or wife recognized the charred remains of a loved one, and the woman wept as only a woman can weep.

Keeper McGuire, who has witnessed much sorrow in his place, and who is supposed to have a heart of adamant, wiped tears from his eyes, and then tried to excuse himself by saying: "This is too much. I am almost unnerved."

Occasionally some plain, methodical person entered, and, through close searching, discovered one who was known to him. In a business-like way the discoverer pinned a card or a slip of paper, bearing the man's name, to what remained of the clothing. Young and giddy girls, who should have been chastised for their impudence, flaunted themselves in the presence of distressed visitors, and seemed to enjoy their trip through the Morgue.

On each side of the building is a yard, and there are many windows. Small boys and stalwart men peered through these windows and indulged in expressions that were unseemly. This outside rabble became so unruly that an additional force of police was called upon to prevent a crush into the building.

None of the bodies were put on the slabs. All were on the flooring. The faces were so blackened by the fire that they could not be recognized, and it was only through clothing or jewelry that any were identified. The undertakers of Brooklyn combined together and volunteered their services in behalf of the sorrow-stricken families. They were of very great assistance to the police in preventing professional mourners from robbing the dead. One woman recognized her brother when she discovered a stud in his shirt bosom. Another woman, with a small piece of cloth and a piece of shirt bosom, identified her husband, and saying, "He has $100 in his pockets," put her hand in his vest pocket and took therefrom that amount.

The arms of nearly all the dead were fixed as though shielding their faces, and one woman had drawn her clothing over her face and clinched her hands above her forehead. Two young men were grappled together as though they had had a personal encounter in an attempt to escape from the theatre. Others lay on their sides in the manner of persons who thus slumber. Their watch chains and other jewelry were beautifully bright, and the clothing of all was blackened through the fire.

In only about one-third of the cases were the limbs exposed through the torn and burned clothing. Uplifted hands, whose fingers were shining bones, bore golden rings, and shoeless feet glistened in their whiteness. The hair and whiskers were gone, and faces were terribly scarred. A few of the bodies were burned to a crisp, and these were put into rough pine boxes, and all hope for their identification was given up.

Until late in the afternoon, men, women, and children flocked to the Washington street station to tell of fathers, husbands, brothers, and children who had not returned to their homes since the evening previous. Hour by hour the list of missing persons increased in numbers until it comprised nearly 200 names. All who made inquiry for friends or relatives were necessarily disappointed, for the blackened, charred bodies were few of them in a condition to be identified. Strong men, who had kept up both heart and hope, broke down and sobbed like women when they learned their own flesh and blood might never be discovered from out of the scores of shapeless trunks that were being exhumed from the ruins. Women came in sobbing and went away convulsed with grief. The policemen themselves often surrendered their forced self-possession and sobbed aloud.

In the evening the work was continued by the aid of calcium lights. It was thought best to discontinue the removal of the bodies from the rear through Theatre alley to Myrtle avenue. Sixty-seven in all had been taken out that way. The main entrance, with the ghastly burdens still regularly coming out of it, was thrown into bold relief. The burner and lantern had been knocked off the street lamp over the way, and a great flame of gas blazed and flared into the air, lighting up the scorched and splintered doorway and the upturned faces of the throng. A calcium light on the sidewalk near the door illumined the corridor to the point where the floor had broken, and there another was fixed whose rays shone directly into the deep pit in which the earlier search had discovered the horrible mass of charred human bodies.

This pit was the cellar of the main corridor, and its ruins were separated from the debris in the auditorium by the strong foundation wall that had borne the gallery columns. It was not until nine o'clock that this cellar, about twelve feet wide, and running through to the foundation wall on the alley side, was cleared. Over one hundred and fifty bodies had been removed from it.

Toward the rear fewer were found, and those were evidently not from the gallery, as fragments of kid gloves could be seen on the fingers of the blackened hands, some of which still clutched opera-glasses. These bodies were more thoroughly calcined than those first found, and not unfrequently the firemen were able to put two or three into one box.

After dark the orders against admitting outsiders to the ruins were more strictly enforced. Among those admitted was the foreman of the Grand Jury, W. W. Shumway. A calcium light from the alley wall shone over the ruins of the auditorium, and here the firemen began work shortly after nine o'clock. In addition to the lime light, oil lamps with reflectors and lanterns were used.

In this fitful glare the firemen, their faces pallid from fatigue and hunger, toiled on without a word. The first body found in the auditorium was on the Theatre alley side. Its position indicates that the victim had reached a window when he was struck down.

Some friends of Mr. Murdoch were very anxious that an early effort should be made to recover his body. His mother was expected to arrive in the city during the evening, he having sent for her a few days before. About nine o'clock a stream of water was put upon the ruins in the northeast corner to cool the immense pile of bricks under which the body was thought to lie.

The firemen were greatly impeded by the clouds of steam. They made their way from the southern end toward the stage. The broken wall lay in great lumps of brick and mortar. About halfway toward the stage shapeless human flesh was found crushed between two huge masses which had protected it from the flames that had consumed all the rest of the body. It was long before the bricks could be sufficiently cooled to admit the removal of this fragment. It was feared all the bodies in this part of the ruins had been similarly or more thoroughly consumed, owing to the intense heat from the inflammable stage fixtures.

The interior of the Adams Street Market presented at night a weirdly horrible sight. Disuse had made the place grimy. The gas fixtures had been removed, and candle light had to be used. The bodies were in rows that reached the entire length of the long apartment. On the breast of each was a lighted candle held in a small block of wood. Candles were also stuck on the hooks that had once been used to hang meat on, and lanterns helped to illuminate the spacious place ; but the combined light was not sufficient to rid the corners of dark shadows. The bodies were in strained shapes, as though death had stopped them in a writhing struggle. Their arms were raised to their faces in most instances, the gesture suggesting suffocation or warding off heat. The charring made them appalling to look at. At an old counter officers added to lists the names of the few who were from time to time identified.

Articles taken from the bodies were in a basket, enveloped and numbered, and corresponding numbers were written on slips of paper and pinned to the rags that still clung to the corpses. Men and women passed from body to body, seeking friends or relatives, examining the bits of clothing, holding the candles close to the blackened faces, and looking for scars or other marks that might make recognition possible. They were wonderfully composed in manner, the only outbreaks of feeling being when a search was successful, and that was very rare. They were in the main of the poor class, such as occupy the galleries of theatres. They were persistent in their sad task, going along the rows of ill-shapen remains without missing a thing that promised identification. In several instances importunate appeals were made for permission to remove recognized remains, but the coroners decided not to grant that privilege until the next day.

On the next morning (December 7th) the confusion was less at the scene of the awful catastrophe, but the solemn gloom was deeper than before, the excitement was nearly as great, and the under-currents of sympathy more intense. There was a gloom in Brooklyn which could be felt even in the streets. There was but one topic of conversation. Men, women, and children thought and talked of little else than the Brooklyn Theatre and the burned dead beneath it ruins. On the sidewalks, in the street-cars, on the ferry-boats, there was one and the same subject of interest. In the neighborhood of the theatre itself the excitement was at its height. But there was little to be seen that could either stimulate or gratify curiosity. Two or three undertakers' wagons with the ugly coffins from the dead-house, were in attendance, but the uninterrupted procession of corpses, which was so horrible a feature of the scene on Wednesday, ended late at night, and on this morning there was nothing to see save the smouldering ruins of the theatre. There was only the great void where the theatre had stood, a mere rim of crumbling walls, scarcely breast high, enclosing immense heaps of brick and rubbish, from which columns of steam arose in the air.

A surging mass of people occupied the sidewalk in front of the deadhouse, and stretched into the middle of the street, and men and boys clambered upon fences and wagons in the neighborhood, and gazed intently at the blank walls of the building. Policemen guarded the main entrance and the iron gateway before it. No permits for admission were demanded of those persons who could satisfy the officers that they had lost friends or relatives by the fire. They were allowed to enter from time to time, passing in the front door and through the room on the right-hand, which contained about thirty bodies, lying on the floor, none of them identified; so, through a smaller room at the further end of the building, back to the left-hand room, in which some of the corpses were lying upon marble slabs and tables in the centre. Upon such bits of clothing as remained upon the bodies, numbers, written hastily with lead-pencils on bits of paper, had been pinned; and where a body had been recognized, the name and address were added to the number. Then, upon receipt of the coroner's permission, the corpse was placed in a plain deal coffin and sent to the address given by the persons who had claimed it.

On Friday morning (December 8th) the work of removing and examining the ruins was suspended, it being deemed unsafe to proceed any further while the walls remained in such an unsafe position. The dangerous parts of the walls were, however, braced, and the firemen resumed their labors in the afternoon.

During Friday night and early Saturday morning a large number of small pieces of bodies, and several heads, were discovered, and the trunk of a body which was identified as that of Mr. Murdoch. The remains were taken in charge by an undertaker.

Many of the bodies were so mangled and charred that it was impossible to identify them, and it was determined by the Board of Aldermen to bury these at the public expense. The scenes at the Morgue and the old market on Saturday morning were, if possible, more heart-rending and horrible than anything that had occurred in those places since the burning of the theatre. The undertakers' wagons rattled up to the door of the old market by dozens,

Identifying the Bodies in the Morgue.
Identifizirung der Leichen in der Morgue.

and the coffins of stained and polished wood, studded with silver nails, were ranged in rows on the market floor, beside the black, gnarled things that had been human bodies. Outside a motley crowd of men, women, and boys pressed close to the doors and tried to get past the police lines in order to witness the work of putting the stiffened and distorted bodies into the narrow coffins. Wandering among the ghastly rows was the usual throng of sight-seers and mourners searching for friends.

Soon after one o'clock the last coffin was taken from the old market, and the driver who carried it hurried away after the others. The crowd around the door took a last glance at the blackened floors inside, as though the horrible place had fascinated them, and then chased the wagons and carriages that were going to join the procession.

The Funeral.

At a quarter before two o'clock the gleam of bayonets appeared in Scher-merhorn street, and the winds bore fitfully the strains of a dirge played by a military band. The head of the procession was nearing the point of estab-lishment of the right of the line. At Flatbush avenue it halted for ten minutes only, while the disposition of the various parts of the procession was perfected. The Twenty-third Regiment, that had marched up in hollow square formation, opened and rested at an "order arms," while the Forty-seventh Regiment passed through and took the right of the line, headed by its splendid band. Then the hearses and undertakers' wagons were broken from single to double column, and the Twenty-third Regiment was placed as a guard of honor, surrounding this portion of the mournful cortege. The other necessary dispositions were quickly effected, and then the march was resumed, with the procession in the following order:

Squad of Mounted Police—Sergeant Johnson.
Alderman Fisher and Supervisor Quimby of Committees—in carriage.
Forty-seventh Regiment Band.
Forty-seventh Regiment.
Detachment Fourteenth Regiment, without arms.
Gatling Battery, without piece.
Conterno's Band.
Twenty-third Regiment as Guard of Honor, leading and flanking first hearses.
Hearses—Seventeen.
Forty-five Undertakers' Wagons, with from one to four coffins each.
Carriages with Relatives and Friends.
Carriages with Ministers and Officials.
Thirteenth Regiment and Drum Corps.

Near Bergen street the dirge which the band had been playing up to that point ceased, and the roll of twenty-four muffled tenor drums marked the time for the steps of the military. Solemnly impressive as had been the music of the band it seemed infinitely less effective than the roll of the drums. The former had the color of melody, even though full of sadness, but the latter impressed itself on the heart as a monotone of sobs. The air grew heavier with the weight of those measured pulsations of half-voiced grief. Along both side-

3

walks moved steadily, keeping step with the procession, a silent multitude. There was no hurrying, no conversation to beguile the weary way; only a sullen resistance to the frenzy of the gale.

The drums ceased, and from the military band wailed forth another dirge more weirdly sad than that first played. A trembling, thrilling cry, as of a stricken soul, voiced by a single cornet, awoke, a harmonic wail, in hearing which, one could not repress a shudder. Again the music ceased, and the terrible roll of the muffled drums began, mingled with the shriekings of the storm.

The march was a terrible one, for its oppressive gloom, the deadly cold, the grief on every hand; but that portion from Sixth avenue to the gate of Greenwood Cemetery was in all respects the worst. All that way the roll of the muffled drums continued, and across the wide vacant spaces toward the bay the icy blast seemed the breath of death itself.

Battle Hill, where the arrangements for the interment of the bodies in one common grave had already been made, is the highest point of ground in the cemetery, and is situated but a short distance from the gate by which the procession entered. Here a circular trench had been cut, seven feet deep and thirteen feet wide, nearly surrounding a round sodded space ten feet in diameter, upon which the projected monument is to stand.

It soon became evident that human endurance would be insufficient to bear any protraction of the obsequies. With wonderful fortitude, not less than 2,000 persons maintained their places about the enormous grave, held as if by a hideous fascination. But all were suffering intensely from cold, and it was determined by those in charge to make the services as brief as possible.

The Rev. John Parker read the Protestant Episcopal burial service. The Rev. Dr. Putnam, instead of the extended funeral oration which he had prepared for the occasion, announced that the extreme cold would preclude the possibility of its delivery, and merely said a few brief words on the uncertainty of life and the blessed hopes of immortality. Then the benediction was pronounced by the Rev. Mr. Odell, and the ceremony concluded with the singing by the Germania choir of Kuhlau's beautiful choral, "Above all summits there is repose."

Besides the public funeral, many private ones, of persons who had been identified by friends, took place on Saturday, Sunday and Monday.

The bodies of the actors Murdoch and Burroughs were taken to Irving Hall at 1 o'clock on Saturday, and remained in state until the funeral on Sunday.

Great festoons of crape hung in long curves from a common centre in the middle of the room reaching to the galleries, that were draped in funeral cloth. Each end of the hall bore its burden of black. Two circles of gas in the ceiling cast a melancholy radiance. The bodies were encased in two rosewood coffins mounted with silver, which were placed in the centre of the room. The coffins severally bore the inscriptions:

CLAUDE DE BLENAU BURROUGHS,
Born Aug. 12, 1848; died Dec. 5, 1876.

HENRY S. HITCHCOCK,
Died Dec. 5, 1876, aged 31.

Crosses and wreaths, the gifts of friends, covered the lid of each. At their head was placed a stand containing a large scroll of white flowers with the word "Arcadian" in violet, the tribute of the members of the former club of that name. There was also a rich offering from the Order of Elks, with the mystic initials of the order predominant. As soon as the bodies were placed in position friends began to pass by the coffins. They continued to do so in the afternoon and evening. During the night the bodies were watched by a committee, the members of which relieved each other at intervals.

The funeral services were held in the Church of the Transfiguration, better known as "The Little Church Around the Corner." The services were very impressive, and the attendance was very large. Dr. Houghton conducted. The remains of Mr. Burroughs were placed in the receiving vault of the Second Street Cemetery, and those of Mr. Murdoch were taken to Philadelphia, and buried on Monday in Woodland Cemetery, the funeral services being conducted in St. Peter's P. E. Church.

Mr. Murdoch's Career on the Stage.

Mr. Henry S. Murdoch, one of the victims of the terrible calamity, was engaged in the caste of the "Two Orphans" as *Pierre*, the cripple, and was the sole support of a widowed mother and two sisters, who reside in Philadelphia. The latter were expected in Brooklyn next week to visit their brother during the Christmas holidays. Mr. Murdoch was born in Boston, August 5, 1845, and was consequently in the thirty-second year of his age. He received his education in Philadelphia, and made his début at the Arch Street Theatre, in that city, in the winter of 1864. During the season of 1865 he fulfilled an engagement at the Boston Museum, and from there he went to Cincinnati, where he performed at Pike's Opera-house until its destruction by fire on March 22, 1866. In this case he narrowly escaped with his life, and lost his entire wardrobe in the fire. He next went to San Francisco, where he played with John McCullough at the California Theatre. He remained there two years—1867-8. He then performed short engagements in Washington, Baltimore, St. Louis and Pittsburgh. In 1872-3 he played at the Arch Street Theatre, Philadelphia, under the management of Mrs. John Drew, taking the parts of "fop" and "walking gentleman," and upon one or two occasions played leading characters. The season of 1873-4 he spent in Chicago, and acted at Hooley's Theatre, under the management of Mr. Fred Williams, of Boston. He resigned his position before the close of the season to support Miss Clara Morris at the Academy of Music in the same city, then under the management of Mr. C. R. Gardner, who is now the manager of the Arch Street Theatre, Philadelphia, where Mr. Murdoch made his début. During his engagement with Miss Morris he made a decided hit as *Armande*, in the play of "Camille." At the conclusion of his engagement in Chicago he returned to Boston, where he remained one season, and commenced his engagement with Messrs. Shook & Palmer last spring, when he played the part of *Sandy Morton*, in the play of "Two Men of Sandy Bar," at the Union Square Theatre, New York. From there he went to the Brooklyn Theatre on October 9 last. Mr. Murdoch was a nephew of Mr. James E. Murdoch,

the eminent tragedian, and a brother of Frank Murdoch, the author of " Davy
Crockett." He has a brother in New Orleans also an actor, whose stage
name is William Wallace, and who lately made his début in that city. Mr.
Murdoch was an accomplished and educated gentleman, and a rising actor.
During his engagement in Boston he played such characters as *Charles Mid-
dlewick*, in the play of " Our Boys," and *Harry Spreadbrow*, in " Sweethearts."
He gave much satisfaction in Brooklyn in his interpretation of *Eustace*, in
"Conscience," *Charles Surface*, in " School for Scandal," and was giving an
exceptionally good rendition of *Pierre*, the cripple, in the " Two Orphans," at
the time of the fire. He was a good vocalist and amateur artist. He had
been suffering from sciatica for some time, and the malady had given him
considerable pain during the six weeks previous to his tragic death, causing
him to limp painfully at times. He occupied apartments at No. 53 Concord
street, where his uncle, Mr. Henry Murdoch, resides.

Claude Burroughs.

Claude Burroughs first made his appearance on the stage at the Winter
Garden, New York, in 1865, playing in " Hamlet " with Edwin Booth. At
the conclusion of his engagement with Mr. Stuart, who was then managing
the Winter Garden, he went to Brooklyn, where he played light comedy
parts in the Park Theatre, then under Mrs. Conway's management. Upon
the opening of the Union Square Theatre by Messrs. Shook & Palmer Mr.
Burroughs was engaged to play light parts. His first appearance at that
theatre was as a *reporter* in " Agnes," the first piece produced in the house,
and he has been in the caste of nearly every play since produced there.
Upon a few occasions when not playing in New York he has accepted engagements in Brooklyn. He was the fop in " Atherley Court," the fop in " Jane
Eyre," *Maxime* in " Ferreol," and a very clever representative of *Talbot
Champneys* in " Our Boys." At the time of his death he was playing *Picard*,
the valet in the " Two Orphans." Since the opening of the St. Stephen's
Hotel, in Eleventh street, in October, Mr. Burroughs has lived there. He
had a delightful summer residence at Larchmont, on the New Haven Road,
where he was wont to entertain his numerous friends. He was about twenty-
six years of age and unmarried.

Sketches of other Victims.

Stuart Campbell Hand, a young reporter on the staff of the *Commercial
Advertiser* of New York, is among the victims of the calamity. He is known
to have visited the theatre on the night of the fire, and has not been seen
since. He was only eighteen years old.

William L. Donnelly, another young reporter, left his home on the evening of the fire to visit the theatre, and was never seen alive again. He had
just returned to New York from a journalistic trip to the West. Among the
charred remains his stepfather felt assured he had discovered poor Donnelly's
body, identifying it by several articles of clothing; but as these articles were
partly divided between two crisped trunks his mother declined to acquiesce in
the identification, for fear of receiving the wrong body.

Mrs. Caroline Berri and her mother, Mrs. Martin, were undoubtedly trampled upon by the panic-stricken audience, and then fell victims to the flames. Mrs. Berri was the wife of officer Richard Berri, of District-Attorney Britton's office. He accompanied her and Mrs. Martin to the theatre; but when the cry of fire rang through the house, and the audience became uncontrollable, he was standing in the vestibule. He tried to push into the theatre to rescue his relatives, but was carried by the rushing crowd out into the street. His wife and her mother undoubtedly perished together.

Officer Patrick McKean, of the Central Office Squad, who was detailed to preserve order in the gallery of the theatre, is among the dead. He was a good officer, and had been made a member of the Central Squad for his exemplary conduct. He was seen working bravely in the vestibule of the theatre, trying to get the panic-stricken people to move out in an orderly manner. Just before the fatal blast of smoke and gas filled the entire building it was noticed that he was exhausted by his hard labors; that he had lost his hat, and that his coat was torn from him by the surging crowd. It is supposed that he was precipitated, when the flooring gave way, into the horrible pit from which so many dead were taken on Wednesday. Officer McKean was a young man—about thirty years of age, and the support of a widowed mother.

John McGinniss, an old employee of the Brooklyn *Eagle*, was among the killed, with two lady friends whom he had escorted to the theatre. He was about thirty-five years old, and was well known in Brooklyn. It is likely that he bravely remained with his lady friends until the last. He was an old fireman of the former volunteer department, accustomed to battling with flames, cool-headed, and rapid in decision, and if he had been alone would undoubtedly have found means of escape.

The body of Nicholas F. Kelly, aged twenty-two, was taken out of the theatre early Wednesday morning. As it was being placed in an undertaker's wagon a young man standing by glanced at the corpse, and after saying, "My God, that's Father Kelly's brother," fainted away. The body was afterward identified by Father Kelly himself, who is the pastor of the Church of the Visitation, and one of the best-loved and most eloquent priests in Brooklyn.

Almost Incredible.

The following story would be deemed almost incredible were it not vouched for by Police Captain Worth. Mr. Hecht, of 431 Pulaski street, a wealthy merchant, identified the remains of his son, Louis, eighteen years old, by the gold watch and gold chain and seal-skin hat found on the remains. As he stood stricken with grief over the charred corpse, two men jostled him aside, and, with many exclamations of sorrow and grief, claimed the body as that of their relative, and looked about for means to remove it. When the grief-stricken parent recovered from the shock their positive identification gave him, he again examined the body, and satisfying himself that they were those of his son, he directed their attention to the marks and signs by which he declared it impossible for him to be mistaken. The men passed away. They, however, were followed by others. To these the father again rehearsed his story of identification. " I thought," said Mr. Hecht, speaking to Coroner Nolan, " that the people were mistaken in the identification of the remains, but when over half a dozen people, whom I saw by their actions had no one among the unfortunates, came along, and with pretended cries of grief pointed out the body as that of some relative, I knew that it was done for the sake of obtaining possession of the valuables."

Mr. Hecht, before seeking out the coroner to obtain a permit for the removal of the body, placed his son, the dead boy's brother, guard over the remains. The coroner at once made all the necessary arrangements to offset the work of these fiends.

The History of the Brooklyn Theatre.

In 1871 a building association, composed in chief of Wm. C. Kingsley, Alexander McCue, and Abner C. Keeney, erected for Mrs. F. B. Conway the edifice then known as " Mrs. Conway's Brooklyn Theatre." Under her management the first season opened on the evening of October 2d, 1871, the play being Bulwer's comedy of " Money," with Mr. and Mrs. Conway, Edward Lamb, Mrs. Farren, and others in the cast. Until 1875, with varying success, Mrs. Conway kept the theatre open, introducing her daughters, Minnie (now Mrs. Levy) and Lilian, Mr. Roche, Mr. Lamb, Mr. Chippendale, Mrs. Farren and others, in the regular company, and playing as occasional stars, Booth, Raymond, Jefferson, Sothern, the Florences, the Williamses, and Charlotte Thompson. At her death the daughters continued the lease, making their managerial debut in " The Two Orphans." The house was packed, and when *Henriette* said to the blind *Louise*, " Don't say so, dear sister; we are not without friends, I hope," the audience rose as with a single impulse, and for five minutes stopped the action of the play by demonstrations as wild as they were encouraging. It soon became evident, however, that the Conway element could not make the theatre a success, and a lease was issued to Sheridan Shook and A. M. Palmer, of the New York Union Square Theatre. Under their management as a star and stock theatre it soon became a popular resort. But perhaps the greatest success the theatre has known was the " Two Orphans," the strongest play of the century, which ran hundreds of nights in New York, and with almost equal favor was played in Brooklyn.

The conveniences in the auditorium of the Brooklyn Theatre were admirably arranged for ingress and comfort, but for egress and safety they were like those of every other theatre. The outer entrance was shut off from the street by three doors. Two of these opened on to a corridor, on the left of which was the box office, and at the further end the ticket-taker's stand, with movable doors, kept shut until a few moments before the close of the performance. An orderly and an unexcited audience would have no difficulty in getting out, for there were two large doors opening from the first circle on to the corridor, which in turn led to the movable doors referred to. The third door at the front entrance opened on a short and narrow hall, on one side of which was the party wall, and on the other a high iron partition. From this hall one

fire followed us fast, and there was still a crowd of excited people to pass through. We got into the crowd and dashed along, heedless that now and again we felt that we had trod upon a human being. Once I looked down and saw a human face, horribly distorted and burned. Oh, my God! it was a fearful sight. I shall never forget it. Afterward I saw the injured man taken out. He was horribly injured, and I think, must be dead. As soon as we got into the street we dashed into the police station. There a gentleman loaned me his overcoat, and after a short stay in the station we walked around home."

Escaping through the Grating.

William Kerr, of Hamden street, Brooklyn, says that he was in front of the theatre when the fire broke out. He attempted to enter the theatre, but was prevented, and stepping back to the street he heard a noise beneath the sidewalk. The iron plate over the coal-hole was pushed up, and the head and shoulders of a man appeared. He pulled the man to the sidewalk, and he was followed by another man. He was then ordered off by the police. The police clapped the plate back, and nothing is known of the fate of the men who went back.

Mad Struggles for Life.

When the rush from the parquet was at its height a father and mother with their child had made their way as far as the lobby, when the father, who held the child in his arms, was knocked down by the crowd. The child fell with its father, and its cries could be heard above all the din. The father struggled to his feet, and as he arose with the child in his grasp, the blood flowed from several gashes in his face and crimsoned his shirt. At the sight of the blood the wife shrieked and immediately fainted, falling upon the people directly in front of her. Two men who appeared to think less of themselves than of others, lifted her up, and after a desperate struggle succeeded in removing her to the street, thence to the police station, where she was afterward joined by her husband and child. The man was found to have been badly injured by being trampled upon, beside being cut about the face.

In another instance a wife became separated from her husband. The husband had fallen beneath the feet of the crowd, and his face was trampled into an almost unrecognizable mass. The woman became frenzied and clutching her hat tore it from her head. Few people paid any attention to her. Her cries were heard on the street.

" Where is my husband ?" she shrieked. " Where is my husband? Won't some one find him for me? My God! my God! I shall go mad."

People thought

She Was Already Mad.

The nearly lifeless form of her husband was subsequently dragged from beneath the feet of the throng and borne into the police station.

A fashionably-dressed lady, who occupied a seat near the stage, was so completely overcome by terror that she sank to the floor, not in a faint, but out of sheer fright. She was actually carried from the place by her attendant.

A Family Almost Blotted Out.

Samuel Solomon told the following sad story at the Morgue, the morning after the fire: "Last night my father, Morris Solomon, my brother Philip, his wife, Lena, and my two sisters, Mary and Deborah, went to the Brooklyn Theatre, and occupied seats in the family circle. When the fire broke out I came up here. The theatre was then in flames. I could see nothing of my relatives. I have remained here all night, with the exception of going home occasionally to see if they had returned. My mother is almost crazy, and has searched our neighborhood for them. Not the slightest trace of either of them has been found since they entered the theatre. I am told the staircase gave way, and I am afraid they have been crushed to death and then burned." The young man was much overcome by the sudden catastrophe which had befallen his family, and shed tears as he recited the story. The missing members of the Solomon family are Morris Solomon, aged 47 years, a cigar dealer at Maiden lane, New York; Philip Solomon, a musician, aged 24; Lena Solomon, his wife, aged 22; Mary Solomon, aged 23, and Deborah Solomon, aged 20 years.

The Numbers in the Theatre.

We have obtained from the returns of the Treasurer what we believe to be a correct list of all who were in the theatre on the night of the fire as spectators, and have also procured a full list of the employees.

In the dress circle	300
In the parquet	250
In the gallery	405
Actors and actresses	21
Supernumeraries	20
Scene shifters and the like	10
Orchestra	12
Dressers, ushers, check takers, etc., etc	22
In all about	1,040

Although it is generally presumed that places of amusement are more apt to be crowded and more subject to fires than churches, history shows that fires in churches have proved even more fatal to human life than all the theatres that were ever burned.

On the 27th of May, 1875, a shocking catastrophe happened in the French Catholic Church, at South Holyoke, Massachusetts, which in many respects was much like that in Brooklyn. The vesper hymn was being sung, when a candle at the altar set fire to the draperies surrounding the image of the Virgin Mary. There were about seven hundred people present, of whom those in the body of the church escaped without difficulty. But the flames streamed upwards to the galleries and spread along them, while the crowd on the staircase became a densely-packed, panic-stricken mass. Many were killed or severely wounded in the crush, besides those who were overtaken by the flames and burned to death. The whole thing lasted but twenty minutes, and in that time over seventy lives were lost.

One of the most terrible disasters of modern times, also strikingly similar to this recent disaster, occurred in the Church of the Jesuits, at Santiago, in Chili, on the 8th of December, 1863. It was the last day of the celebration of the feast of the Immaculate Conception, and the church had been elaborately decorated for the performance of mass.

A gigantic image of the Virgin, in whose honor the celebration was held, occupied a prominent position in the church, and all around pasteboard devices and thickly intertwining draperies covered the masonry of the church from floor to ceiling. Festoons led from pillar to pillar, and from the roof and projecting arches hung twenty thousand paraffine lamps. The women of Santiago, who on these occasions go from church to church, had filled the Church of the Jesuits. Three thousand persons, the greater number of whom were women and children, were present in this most venerable of Santiago's churches, and even on the steps outside women knelt in prayer to the Virgin, whose altar they were unable to reach. In the midst of the ceremony a paraffine lamp burst, and the flames at once caught the draperies and festoons surrounding it. Then from arch to arch and pillar to pillar the fire leaped, the lines that held the lamps aloft being burned the burning paraffine was emptied on the women below; and, while these twenty thousand vessels of flaming liquid were deluging the unfortunate women, the decorations above carried the flames to the roof, which burned and crackled like a tinder-box.

A rush was made for the great centre door, and in a few minutes it was hopelessly blocked, while only a few knew of the small door beyond the altar. As women endeavored to escape through the crowd, others who were burning clutched their dresses and cried in piteous tones for help, and clinging in their agony communicated the flame that was consuming them to the persons whom they had seized. Some women in their desperation divested themselves of their clothing, and a few succeeded in effecting their escape, but only a few. Each moment increased the crowd and intensified the block at the main door, and while it became more and more difficult to escape, the flames were spreading on the floor, flying from one prostrate body to another, and destroying the panic-stricken creatures by scores and hundreds, while the church resounded with piteous cries for help and still more heartrending shrieks of agony; the vast roof now gave way, and came down with its blazing beams and rafters, crushing and inundating the seething mass of tortured individuals beneath it. When the fire had burned itself out and workmen could get at the ruins, two thousand corpses were carried out.

Relief for the Destitute.

As soon as it was known that so many had perished in the flames, a generous spirit of rivalry sprang up among the proprietors of places of amusement all over the country, as to whom should contribute the largest amount of money for the relief of the survivors and those rendered destitute by the fire. Individual actors also subscribed liberally, and a relief association was organized to receive and disburse the money thus contributed. Memorial services were held in New York and Brooklyn the Sunday after the fire, and prominent clergymen all over the country selected the terrible catastrophe as a theme for eloquent sermons.

Thrilling Account of the Daring Bravery and Wonderful Escape from a Horrible Death of

CORNELIUS J. DALY AND MISS NETTIE MORGAN.

It is a fact greatly to the credit of all present in the terrible fire that but one single case of selfish cowardice was displayed, either by the actors or the audience. Great and noble deeds of daring, loving sacrifices, and humanitarian actions are everywhere described. The daily newspapers have given their readers many instances of true bravery displayed by men and women holding prominent positions in the world, but it remains for the writer to be the chronicler of a series of more daring acts and wonderful escapes, and the historian of two people who passed through the ordeal of fire, one of whom deserves a place high in the record of "brave men who did brave deeds."

The Hero and Heroine.

Cornelius J. Daly, the hero of this sketch, was of humble parentage. The elder Daly, fully appreciating the disadvantages of his own position, early determined that his only son should receive a superior education.

As a consequence, Cornelius—or, as he was more familiarly called, Conn—was sent to school at an early age, and on his seventeenth birthday was in a condition to fairly combat the world and achieve success. He was comely of feature, athletic of frame, and intelligent of mind. He was the pride of his old father and mother, and the admiration of all the friends of the family.

One day Conn returned to his humble home from school to find terror and grief supplanting the usual greeting of joy and pleasure; his father had been brought home in a helpless condition, a victim of the dreaded paralysis. It was evident, now that the head of the family had been incapacitated from further labor, that Conn must do something toward their support.

Throwing to one side all his cherished ambitions and boyish hopes, Conn left school and apprenticed himself in a large machine shop located in Brooklyn. His wages at first were small, but being strong of limb and stout of heart, backed by intelligence, he speedily progressed, and in less than two years was promoted to the position of journeyman. His wages sufficed to keep his father and mother in comparative comfort, but even this failed to satisfy him. He yearned for something higher and nobler, and after working a few months as a journeyman, he grew dissatisfied with his position. He loved his old father and mother with all the ardor of his warm generous heart, and he feared lest lack of means should compel him to abridge their enjoyment of little luxuries he deemed necessary for their declining years.

Again, Conn was in love, but when he reflected over this last situation his heart sank even lower than when contemplating his pecuniary distress. It

Rescuing her paralyzed Father.
Errettung ihres gichtbrüchigen Vaters.

was the old, old story of honest, manly poverty, loving the daughter of proud and pampered wealth. Conn was employed in a large machine shop, owned by a wealthy resident of Brooklyn.

It chanced one day that the proprietor's beautiful daughter, Nettie, visited her father's establishment, and not finding him in the business office sought him among the workmen. Mr. Morgan was in the act of giving Conn some instructions in reference to a piece of work when the rich young beauty approached him, and with girlish impetuousness began questioning about the to her wonderful mysteries of the tools and machinery about her. The indulgent father, after mildly chiding her for thus venturing among the oil-begrimed machinery, turned to Conn, who had stood awe-stricken before the beautiful young girl, and said:

"Daily, this is my daughter, Miss Nettie. She desires to learn something of the uses to which the machinery is applied. Show her around the shop."

At the sound of his employer's voice Conn recovered a portion of his senses, and, blushing and bowing toward the radiant beauty, who flashed the brilliancy of her black eyes full upon him, muttered some incoherent response, and waited for the young lady's commands.

Mr. Morgan walked away toward his office, and Miss Nettie's manner toward the young mechanic was so kind that his first confusion melted away like snow before the summer sun, and in five minutes the beautiful heiress and the hard-handed mechanic were chatting together with the familiarity of old acquaintances.

Miss Morgan seemed determined to learn all the details of the business, and Conn was only too pleased to instruct her in the use and appliance of the tools and machinery.

All pleasant things must some time have an ending, and the tour of the shop was at last completed. It had taken them nearly two hours to go through, however, and Conn would have been the happiest of mortals if he could have had the privilege of being Miss Nettie's conductor and instructor forever.

"Good-by, Mr. Daly," murmured Miss Nettie, extending her aristocratic hand, white as alabaster, toward our hero, when the inspection of the machinery was at last completed. "Good-by. I am ever so much obliged to you."

It was, undoubtedly, very foolish and very improper, but when those dainty fingers touched his palm Conn caught them up and, bending over, kissed the little hand with the courtly grace of a cavalier. Miss Nettie blushed, but did not seek to prevent this delicate homage, and with another "Good-by," tripped away, while poor Conn's head whirled around more rapidly than did the fly-wheel of the great engine.

This was the beginning, and all the remainder of that day and the next and the next Conn saw nothing, could think of nothing but Miss Nettie Morgan. He lost his appetite, grew moody, shunned companionship with his fellow-workmen, and it is positively asserted that on more than one occasion he secreted himself in the vicinity of the Morgan mansion to feast his eyes, if possible, on the person of his lady-love idol.

Once he met her in the street. She was just stepping from her father's

4

carriage, attired in silk and velvet, and poor Conn, in his ordinary work clothes, was going from his dinner to the shop. His heart gave a great jump when he saw her, and then his brain reeled and he felt sick and faint. Miss Nettie turned to give some instructions to the coachman and her eyes fell upon Conn. Instantly she stopped, and going toward him a step, extended her hand and said :

" Mr. Daly, don't you know me ? Were you going by without speaking ? How have you been ? "

Again Conn experienced the electric thrill shot from those white taper fingers, and once again his heart leaped so joyfully that it nearly choked him He contented himself this time with bowing very low, and pressing her hand very slightly for just one blissful second. Then she passed into a store, and Conn, with a dazed feeling of happiness, went on down the street.

But why linger over a description of this love feeling ? All of us experience it at some time in our life, and I opine it is a glorious experience, and marks an epoch in life. Conn's employer became cognizant of this state of affairs. Angered at the " impudence " of the " beggar," as he contemptuously termed our hero and his passion, he immediately discharged him, and then Conn's worship of Miss Nettie assumed the most lowly type of idolatry. He would have been content to do her humble service all his life, provided she spoke kindly and extended her hand to him but once a year. He lingered around her father's house at all hours now, day and night, and such persistent and mysterious watching of one house made him an object of suspicion to the police. He saw her very frequently, but at a distance. He felt sure that it would always be at a distance he might worship her, but it was pleasant— nay, bliss supreme—to sometimes hug the delusive " might be," and build brighter and airier castles.

A few days after his discharge Conn made the acquaintance of a representative of the Peruvian government, interested largely in the railroad development of his country. The gentleman was at once impressed with the self-reliant intelligence of our hero, and finding him conversant with the intricate details of machine construction engaged him at a munificent salary to superintend the locomotive and machine works of the Peruvian government, then in process of erection at Valparaiso.

It was demanded by his new employer that he proceed to the field of his future operations immediately, and a steamer leaving that day Conn could only communicate with his beloved parents by letter, informing them of his good fortune.

When Miss Nettie learned that Conn had been discharged she took especial pains to make inquiries about him and his future. She never confided to any one her feelings toward the young man, but it must be admitted that she felt a tender interest in his welfare, and now that he was gone, missed his handsome face sorely.

A Lapse of Years.

This was in 1871, and Conn was in his twenty-second year. As the steamer bearing him away left his native shores in the dim distance, he lifted up a prayer to the Most High to guide him aright in his new undertaking, and he inwardly resolved that he would some day return socially the equal of the girl he loved. He could then dare to ask her hand in marriage.

Five years passed away, spent by our hero in a persistent, laborious struggle toward the goal he had marked in life. His efforts were rewarded, and he had not been long among the indolent Chilians before his superior strength of intellect lifted him above all competitors, and a stream of wealth steadily poured toward him. A great railroad was projected, and Conn—we still preserve the familiar title—had the sole contract to build and equip it. The determination was to provide the travelling public with all manner of modern conveniences, and to encourage home industries, car and locomotive works, rolling mills, machine shops, etc., were established, and Conn started for home to engage skilled labor in all the different departments.

He arived safely in Brooklyn, and at once proceeded towards his old home, his heart overflowing with joy as he fancied the surprise and rejoicing of his parents at his unexpected return. The old house looked doubly familiar as he approached it, but no welcome light shone from the windows. He knocked long and loudly at the door, but receiving no response he was about turning away, when a woman in an adjoining house raised the window and asked him what he desired.

"I was in search of Mr. and Mrs. Daly," said Conn. "Can you tell me if they still live here?"

"They still live here," replied the woman, "but they went to New York early this morning to visit some friends, and will not be back until to-morrow."

Thanking the woman for this information Conn turned away, and with aimless steps walked down the street. He passed a theatre, resplendent with light, and joined the throng of gayly-dressed pleasure-seekers, filing into the building. He asked for a ticket at the box-office, but was told that all reserved seats had been taken, and that only gallery tickets were procurable.

"That will do," he said, and, taking the bit of pasteboard entitling him to a seat, passed up the long, winding stairs to the gallery, and took a position in the front row of seats.

It was a remarkable concidence that Miss Nettie Morgan had accepted an invitation to visit the same theatre that evening. Mr. George St. Clair Fitzherbert, a young gentleman of elegant leisure, considerable wealth and few brains—nevertheless aristocratically connected, and therefore a welcome visitor at the Morgan mansion—had purchased two orchestra seats in the most eligible locality, and invited Miss Nettie to do him the honor of sharing one of them. Now Nettie failed to have a very high regard for George St. Clair Fitzherbert's aristocratic connections, leisurely habits, wealth, etc.; in fact she had been known to call him a "conceited booby," but Miss Nettie was fond of the theatre; she very much desired to see the "Two Orphans," and therefore did the young scion of aristocracy "the honor."

The interval before the appearance of the orchestra was devoted by Conn to a careful survey of the theatre and the audience. Just as the overture began Miss Nettie and her aristocratic escort entered, and the former was immediately recognized by Conn. Instantly all interest in the play was lost. He had eyes and thoughts only for Nettie Morgan. If one had asked Conn the next day the simplest question about the play, it is doubtful if he could have answered it. Miss Nettie, unconscious of this idolatrous adorer's silent, soul-enraptured worship, gave all her sympathies to the troubles and heart-griefs of the "Two Orphans." More than once tears sprang to her eyes at the pathetic situations.   •

The Cry of Fire.

The curtain was rung up on the last scene of the last act. It was the hut of the *Frochards* on the bank of the river Seine. It discovered the blind girl *Louise* on her pallet of straw, over whom was bending *Pierre Frochard*. Suddenly the actors heard whispers of "Fire, fire," and a shuffling to and fro behind the scenery. Mr. Murdoch, who was playing *Pierre*, also heard the alarm, and Miss Claxton (*Louise*) whispered to him:

"The stage is on fire!"

The play went on, *Louise* and *Pierre* continuing to recite their parts. When Mrs. Farren, as *Pierre's* mother, rushed in and, as the action of the play demanded, seized *Louise* by the hair and pulled her head violently back-ward, Miss Claxton's eyes were turned upward, and then she saw little tongues of flame playing over her head and licking up the flies at the top of the scenes. There were now four persons on the stage: Miss Claxton, Mrs. Farren, J. B. Studley and H. S. Murdoch.

As they went on with the play, they whispered to one another about the fire and exhorted one another to do everything possible to prevent a panic in the audience. They thought that the flames might yet be extinguished with-out consuming the stage, and Miss Claxton said to Mr. Murdoch:

"Go on, go on, or there'll be a panic. They'll put the fire out from behind."

In the latter part of the scene, where *Pierre* approaches *Louise*, and she draws back, exclaiming, "I forbid you to touch me!" Mr. Studley, as *Pierre*, turned his back to the audience upon approaching Miss Claxton, and whis-pered to her, while the burning beams above were almost ready to fall upon them, and they knew it:

"Be quiet! Stand perfectly still!" and extending his arms, Miss Claxton remained immovable.

The audience had not yet discovered the fire; but after the passionate ex-clamation, "I forbid you to touch me!" Miss Claxton glanced upward at the roaring flames that were now leaping from scene to scene, and hesitated, un-certain what to do. At this moment those sitting in the body of the house caught sight of the red flames at the top of the stage. Instantly wild cries of "Fire!" Fire!" were heard, and the people sprang to their feet terrified, and rushed, stumbling over the seats and crushing one another, toward the entrance.

Cinders were then falling upon the stage, and Miss Claxton, Mrs. Farren, Mr. Murdoch, and Mr. Studley advanced together to the footlights with panic written on their faces. Mr. Studley, in his stentorian tones, shouted to the affrighted people that they were safe if they kept quiet.

"There will, of course," he said, "be no further performance, but you've all time to get out if you go quietly."

Several persons in the orchestra were recalled to their senses by these words, and they sat down again. The men appeared to be more excited than the women. The aristocratic Fitzherbert, at the first alarm, was seized with a most uncontrollable fear—his blasé face was the color of chalk, and his thin legs knocked together like reeds shaken by the winter wind. Forgetting all else but his own person in a selfish scramble for safety, he started to his feet and was rushing away. Miss Nettie, although terrified beyond measure, had presence of mind enough left to see that haste would only increase the danger. She caught her frightened escort by the hand, and pulled him into the seat beside her.

"Don't run," she cried; "we will get out better if we go slowly."

The musicians in the orchestra were urging the people to retire quietly, and so were the actors. Fitzherbert instinctively turned his eyes toward them, and saw a mass of flame back of the actors, with bits of burning wood dropping down, and the sight seemed to craze him. He started to his feet, tore violently away from Miss Nettie, and dashed into the crowd struggling to escape. The instinct of self-preservation had overcome reason, and the struggle for life became fierce and uncontrollable.

As her escort thus basely deserted her, Nettie's self-possession fled, and with a low moan of anguish she sank back upon the seat and covered her face with her hands.

The Rescue—Facing Death.

Intent on watching Nettie, Conn saw little of the play. When the first cry of "Fire" was raised, he started to his feet and leaned eagerly forward. He saw the sparks falling upon the stage among the actors—heard Miss Claxton cry:

"Will the people keep their seats? We are between you and the flames, and will be burned first. Will the people in the front seats sit down?"

Then he saw the people in the orchestra seats pause for a moment, saw the frightened look on the face of Fitzherbert as Nettie pulled him down beside her, and then, as the coward basely deserted her, he sprang upon the gallery railing, lowered himself to the family circle, from thence down into the body of the house, and in a moment was by the side of the girl he so passionately loved.

She started when he placed his hand upon her shoulder, and then, as her eyes encountered the hungry flames reaching out their long arms, and consuming with lightning rapidity the canvas scenes, hid her face again and shuddered convulsively.

Conn, with his hand still upon her shoulder, looked in the same direction. The beams, supporting the roof of the boat-house, were falling in all directions, and the actors, conscious of their imminent peril, were in the act of rushing from the stage through a perfect rain of fire. As they disappeared a bright tongue of flame shot out over their heads toward the audience. It was like a transformation scene in a spectacle. The musicians were disappearing under the stage. Liberty seemed to lie in that direction.

"Come, Miss Nettie," cried Conn. "We must not perish. I will save you."

She started up with a look of surprise, but uttered no word, and throwing his strong arm around her slender waist, Conn dragged rather than led her toward the little door that gave exit to the musicians. In a moment they were under the stage groping around blindly in the dark, while the angry flame hissed and crackled overhead with a sullen, ominous roar. Supporting the beautiful girl, Conn darted toward a door through which he saw some of the actors disappear. He found himself in a little entry, dimly lighted by a single gas burner. It was a subterranean passage under the floor to the box office in front of the house. Pushing the beautiful girl before him, Conn sprang into this seeming haven of safety, and as the door closed behind him, the angry flames, fanned by the draught, almost licked the clothes from his back. Rapidly fleeing along the passage way, the pair reached a flight of steps, at the head of which was a door. He strove to open it, but his efforts were resisted.

"Great God!" he cried; "it is locked."

Nettie answered with a moan of anguish, and the sight of her face, ethereally beautiful in its paleness, nerved him to desperation. He stepped back a few paces, and threw his entire weight upon the door. It shivered, swayed, and gave way, admitting them into the box office. There was yet another door to pass through, leading into the lobby, through which the maddened multitude was struggling. Resting a moment, Conn again dashed forward and burst the door open against the struggling throng. In an instant the two were in the midst of the frenzied mob, who fought and struggled for life with the desperation of mad men. Men and women were being trampled upon by those behind them, and the former were as terror-stricken as the latter. The glare in the street, and the smoke in the corridor, enhanced the terror of those seeking an exit.

"Cling closely to me," Conn whispered in the ear of the beautiful creature in his arms. Raising aloft his strong right arm, he tightened his hold upon Nettie's waist, and swaying from right to left, fighting down all opposition, was in a minute in the thickest of the throng. The two were lifted off their feet instantly, and carried out into the street with the surging mass.

A carriage was standing near, and into it Conn hurried his half-fainting charge. Directing the coachman to drive with all speed to the address he gave him, Conn leaned again into the carriage, and this time dared to snatch a kiss from her pale lips.

"God bless you, Miss Nettie, my darling!" he cried; and bursting into tears, the beautiful girl could only cry,

"You have saved my life; I shall never forget you."

Again he ventured to touch his lips to her cheek, and then, closing the door of the carriage, he bade the coachman drive with all haste, and hurried back toward the burning theatre.

A mad and frightened crowd was still pouring from the building, and with-

Burning of the Brooklyn Theatre during the performance of the "Two Orphans."
Brand des Brooklyner Theaters während der Vorstellung der „Zwei Waisen."

out one thought of the great danger he placed himself in, Conn dashed in among the struggling men and women, to save more lives, if possible. He struggled manfully with the surging mass, and was soon in the body of the theatre.

But one man and two women were in the auditorium, and bidding them fly for their lives, Conn seized one of the pillars supporting the family circle gallery, and by a few vigorous muscular efforts raised himself to the top of the railing. Jumping quickly over he rushed toward one of the exits, through which a maddened crowd was struggling in tumult and disorder. In vain he endeavored to quell their frenzy. Forcing his way toward the head of the stairs, his strong arm was exerted to hurl back frightened men and allow the shrieking, shouting mass below to escape. Suddenly a cry came from below that aided him to drive back the uppermost.

"For God's sake, turn back ; we cannot get out," was called from the bottom of the blocked and creaking stairway, and immediately there was a momentary relaxation of the downward pressure of the crowd. At this moment Conn extricated himself from the crowd, and hurried back into the dress-circle. The parquet below was empty, and people were dropping from the gallery into it, and lowering themselves from tier to tier. The stage was a mass of flames, and the smoke was filling the auditorium and rushing into the corridors. He hurried to the front main entrance of the dress-circle, and there found a mass of men and women shrieking, shouting and crowding madly down upon the living mass below. For a while the passage seemed blocked by a human barrier which could neither move of itself nor give way to pressure from above. Burly men and weak women seemed alike powerless in that dense throng, and to aggravate the panic, people at the turn of the stairs kept calling, "Go back! go back ! You cannot get out this way." This may have been intended to restrain the crowd above from forcing their way down, but it had a different effect. People madly urged each other forward, men swore and women shrieked, and to heighten the horror of the scene a volume of black smoke burst into the passage and rolled along, blinding the eyes and parching the throat. In this dreadful moment, when the horrors of death seemed to stare those people in the face and to overshadow them like a pall, a desperate flight for life began. Women fainted and men fell under foot and were trampled down, and through that writhing, struggling mass, amid a tumult of cries and shrieks and groans, the lower vestibule was reached.

A lady in front of our hero, pressed and beaten down by the mad crowd, fainted and would have fallen. He caught her in his arms, and now began a desperate struggle. Persons from the gallery and elsewhere had blocked the doors, and there were many behind him in the dress-circle, pushing violently, one even clutching at the head of the unconscious lady as she hung over his shoulder. Slowly they were making for the doors, when the flames from the ceiling seemed to dart down and met the jets from the gaselier. Then there was dreadful yelling and crowding at the doors, men and women struggling desperately for every inch gained. A horrible accident occurred. A lady partly suffocated, like the rest of them, had fallen and could not be lifted, and was evidently trampled to death. But there was no time to think. He passed over several forms. Looking behind for an instant he saw there was a frightful panic in the theatre. The gas or something else had exploded, the lights were out, the flames roared and the pieces of wood and plaster fell upon the heads of those at a distance. "Mercy!" "My God, save me!" and names of husbands and brothers were shouted. The heat was intense, for the fire was rapidly closing upon them. Arms were thrown up in an attempt to force a passage, as men sometimes do when swimming, and dozens must have been swept under and trodden to death. He had now nearly reached the door. All at once a fearful crash came, as if the gallery or ceiling had fallen. "Murder!" "Help!" "Help!" seemed to be shouted from a hundred lips. He turned as he felt the fresh air blow upon his face, and saw behind something like a dark wall. He then felt that at least a hundred and fifty people were shut in to certain destruction. But the groaning and yelling continued worse than ever. Beyond this wall he could see bright flames, which seemed to swell and surge in a terrible manner. On gaining the street he found still more excitement; but he had to hurry to the station-house with his unconscious burden. In a moment he was back again at the theatre, exerting himself to the utmost to quiet the people in the lower lobby, and have them leave in an orderly way, so that all might get out safe. But when the audience, in their mad rush to escape from the flames, began to trample on one another, he commanded them to keep back so that he might save those who had fallen. Although the surging crowd was loath to obey, yet his commands were so earnest that he kept them back a sufficient time to pick up about twenty persons who would otherwise have been crushed and killed, and carried them, comparatively unhurt, into the adjoining station-house. After saving these people he returned to the theatre, which was now enveloped in flames. Men, women and children were thrown down and trampled upon, but the brave man rushed in among the frantic crowd, at the imminent risk of his own life, and pulled out a number of bodies, cut, bruised and bleeding. Those who witnessed his actions state that he saved in this way the lives of at least forty persons.

When the firemen arrived, he assisted them to quell the flames. He remained at the fire throughout the night and all the next day. He was one of the first to discover the dead bodies, and although faint, hungry, and burned and blackened out of human semblance, assisted in getting out the charred and mangled bodies, and it was not until the last one had been removed that he sought repose.

Conclusion.

Conn, or rather Mr. Daly, took an early opportunity of visiting the house of his old employer, Mr. Morgan. Being possessed now of abundant means and letters of introduction from high dignitaries in the Chilian government he had no difficulty in getting an invitation from Mr. Morgan to tea, with whom he had made a large contract for tools.

Miss Nettie looked more charming than ever, and to the surprise of *pater familias* recognized his guest as the brave gentleman who rescued her from the burning theatre. It is unnecessary to say that Mr. Morgan was agreeably surprised, and the gallant rescuer being socially and pecuniarily his peer, young, and distinguished-looking, he began to look upon him as a possible son-in-law.

It was not our purpose to tell a love-story, and it is only necessary to add that if there is anything in "signs," Mr. Daly will certainly carry off as a bride the charming Miss Nettie Morgan.

List of the Sufferers.

It is extremely probable that a great many persons were lost in the terrible fire whose bodies were not recovered. The following is a complete list of the identified dead, the unidentified, and persons reported to the police as missing :

IDENTIFIED.

Argrove, Charles, 152 St. Mark's avenue.
Aurbach, Gustave, 30 Hudson avenue.
Armstrong, Christopher, 208 Skillman street.
Addison, John, 177 Water street.
Aunao, Alfred, 331 Hamilton avenue.
Anand, Gustave, Hamilton avenue.
Athell, Durell, Court and Nelson streets.
Ashwell, Joseph, 86 Fleet street.
Alberte, Amanda, 266 Atlantic avenue.

Bedford, Daniel, Hicks and Clark streets.
Bennett, W., 129 Butler street.
Brook A., 1677 Atlantic avenue.
Brosnan, John, 300 Pearl street, New York.
Brown, William, 520 Hicks street.
Bryant, William A., 107 Flatbush avenue.
Bullion, William F., 436 Lafayette avenue.
Burton, William F., 439 Lafayette avenue.
Bordess, May, 62 Fulton street.
Birdsall, A. B., 334 Atlantic avenue.
Boyle, Peter, Adams place.
Burke, Frederick, 197 Fulton street.
Bolstridge, George, 246 Adams street.
Broderick, Patrick, 85 Sackett street.
Boyle, Thomas, 380 Adams street.
Burroughs, Claude, New York.

Curran, Richard, 123 Jay street.
Clark, E., 135 18th street.
Cowan, James, 68 Sumter street.
Conconan, Peter, 73 Walworth street.
Cinler, John, ——
Chantey, Henry, 289 Court street.
Crandall, William E., 325 Myrtle avenue.
Chichester, T., Baltic street.
Cassidy, M., 475 Adelphi street.

Creech, W., 44 Duffield street.
Cassidy, James, 150 Hamilton avenue.
Conroy, Michael, 256 Plymouth street.
Callom, James, 46 Amity street.
Cassrelt, John, 164 Prince street.
Cowan, James, 197 South Portland avenue.
Cullen, John D., 48 Amity street.
Cullen, James, 41 Amity street.

De Shay, Mr.
Dietz, Aaron, Greene avenue.
Dietz, Abraham, Greene avenue.
Dooner, James, Willoughby and Canton sts.
Devoe, Chas. E., Devoe st., Williamsburgh.
Doner, Hugh, 117 Tillary street.
Dempsey, Thomas, 103 Prince street.
Dorrity, Edward, 103 Prince street.
Deanaro, Clara, 246 Fourth street.
Davidson, Dennis, 26 Withers street.
Dunlan, Charles, 81st street, New York, (supernumerary).
Divine, Thomas, East New York.
Doran, John, Willoughby and Kent aves.
Donlan, William, 171 Prince street.

Elliott, James, Atlantic avenue.
Easebel, John, ——

Fry, John, 316 Skillman street.
Fry, William, 316 Skillman street.
Fry, Henry, 316 Skillman street.
Foley, Cornelius, 151 Degraw street.
Farrell, George, 145 Myrtle avenue.
Franke, Charles, 7 Degraw street.
Franke, William, 129 Columbia street.
Franke, Charles, 129 Columbia street.
Frankish, ——, M. D., ——

Faron, E. E., 54 Charles street.
Farey, Patrick, 104 President street.

Garrett, Charles, 98 Livingstone street.
Gilhoma, Samuel, 138 Portland avenue.
Garvey, John E., 25th street and Third ave.
Goodwin, J., 495 Canal street.
Guthrie, F., 1029 Lafayette avenue.
Glies, Philip, 66 Wolcott street.
Gibbons, Frank, 1029 Lafayette street.
Gray, Alfred H., 158 Calyer street.
Gray, William A., 158 Calyer street.
Guy, James, 128 York street.
Gorth, Frank, ——

Hecht, Louis, 431 Pulaski street.
Hendricks, Mr., 1 Lawrence street.
Hendricks, ——, 191 Fulton street.
Holdrich, Dora.
Holdrich, Emma.
Hartman, William, 2 Myrtle avenue.
Haston, John, 447 Hudson avenue.
Hayes, John, 205 West 22d street.
Hanfry, John, 175 Court street.
Huston, John, 447 Hudson avenue.
Hoefler, George, and child, of Gowanus.
Hoeller, Kate, of Gowanus.
Howell, R., 30 Scholes street.

Jones, Henry H., 154 Summit street.
Jackson, Robert, 443 Flatbush avenue.
Jackson, John A., 355 Adams street.
Jackson, C.

Kerlan, John, Marcy ave. and Koscinsko st.
Kennedy, John, 81 Gold street.
Kraft, Henry, Boerum street.
Kerrigan, Joseph, 341 Water street.   [st.
Kroemer, Joseph, Bushwick ave. and Stagg
Kelly, Michael, 18 Meeker avenue.

Lamb, Lawrence, 311 Plymouth street.
Lane, G.
Lawler, P., 58 Little street.
Lewis, P., Binghampton.
Lowenther, Abram, 203 Fulton street.
Lott, Charles, 464 Sackett street.
Lott, George, 464 Sackett street.
Loughlin, John, 244 Bridge street.
Lassen, Isaac, 264 Atlantic avenue.
Lennon, James, ——
Looney, Joseph, Conover street.
Likewise, Annie, New Lots.
Lohn, John, 186 Prince street.

Martin, Ann and child, 37½ Lawrence st.
McGinniss, John, 38 Little Water street.

McCullough, Angus, 294 Pacific street.
McLoughlin, George, 229 15th street.
McLean, James, 160 Myrtle avenue.
McManus, John, 506 Court street.
McDermott, John, 2 Elliot place.
McCarty, Patrick, 55 James street.
McCafferty, James P., 251 Navy street.
McGiffy, John, 449 Hicks street.
McNally, J., 202 Prince street.
Meeling, J. P., 148 Reardon street.
Meek, J. E., 77 Pacific street.
Martin, P. E., 26 Elliot place.
Morris, J., 22 Liberty street.
Murdoch, H. S., 53 Concord street.
Murphy, James, 62 Amity street.
Murray, William, Navy street.
Mowberry, John, 285 Centre street.
Mitterberry, Diedrich, 551 West 37th. st.
Meigh, Alfred, 89 Bushwick avenue.
Myer, Isaac, New York.

Nagle, W., 58 Broadway.
Neith, C., Smith street.
Nevin, ——, 148 President street.

Offerman, F. D., 16 Smith street.
Osborne, Wm. H., 177 Eagle st., Greenpoint.
Oleson, Louis, 147 Sackett street.
O'Brien, Hugh, 147 Concord street.
Oram, Stephen, 135 Union avenue.
Ostrander, Jacob L., 374 Navy street.

Parsons, Mrs., and child, St. Louis.
Pickford, Frank, Patchen avenue.
Pollard, John, Flushing and Grand ave.
Pearce, W. H., Duffield street.
Phillips, Solomon, ——.

Quinn, James, 81 Gold street.
Quick, Elias B., Jr., 20 8th street, E. D.

Ramsdell, G. R.
Reordon, P., 931 Atlantic avenue.
Ralph, Henry, Grand ave. and Bergen st.
Rogers, Catherine, Snedeker ave., New Lots.

Solomon, Morris, 103 Boerum place.
Solomon, Phillip, 103 Boerum place.
Solomon, Tracey, 103 Boerum place.
Solomon, Lena, 103 Boerum place.
Solomon, Deborah, 103 Boerum place.
Styles, Charles F., 221 Putnam avenue.
Scott, Charles, (officer.)

Taylor, Arthur, 27 Chauncey street.
Turner, John F., Jas and Prospect streets.

Varick, Mrs., ——.

Webster, H., 240 Clinton street.
Wait, A., 80 Bushwick avenue.
Wine, R., 79 Butler street.
Weldon, M. J., 128 South First street.
Whistance, Thomas, 484 Hudson avenue.

Wheeler, Lewis, 147 Sackett street.
Ward, Matilda, 18 Oxford street.
Wakeman, E., Joralemon and Court streets.
Wook, John, 101 Fleet place.

Xendid, William, 161 Fulton street, N. Y.

UNIDENTIFIED OR MISSING.

Arlaum, Arthur, 341 Hamilton avenue.
Alberte, Louis, 266 Atlantic avenue.

Bedford, David, 122 Hicks street.
Binley, John, 56 Box street.
Barnes, ——, 520 Hicks street.
Boyne, Thomas, Vanderbilt avenue.
Ball, William, Third avenue and 36th st.
Ball, George, Third avenue and 36th st. [st.
Blachford, Chas., wife and child, 212 Bridge
Boyne, Bennett, 233 Plymouth street.
Berry, Caroline, Smith street.
Beatty, Edward, 71 Carlton avenue.

Cavanagh, Frost, 474 Hudson avenue.
Crane, Oliver F., 31 North Elliott place.
Collins, Daniel, 101 Prince street.
Chichester, Thomas, 232 Court street.
Coyle, Nicholas, Johnson and Duffield sts.
Cadmos, Mrs. Phil, 628 Fifth avenue.
Cadmos, George W., 628 Fifth avenue.

Deree, Charles E., 34 Devoe street.
Donlan, William, 229 Navy street.
Delepartree, Ed., 66 Smith street.
Dakin, Daniel, New London.
Doolittle, Henry, 153 Union place.

Foden, Walter, 209 Jay street.
Froidevaux, Rosine, 257 Columbia street.
Forskein, Andrew, 1075 Third avenue.

Green, Frank, 1029 Lafayette avenue.
Gregg, John, 251 Van Brunt street.
Gowan, John, 245 Adams street.
Grange, George A., Galveston, Texas.
Game, Robert, 179 Butler street.

Hand, Stewart, Smith and State streets.
Hickey, John, 103 Fulton street.
Hamilton, Delia, Pine and Pearl sts., N. Y.
Harrison, Charles, 349 Bridge street.
Holdridge, George, 245 Adams street.
Haskins, Lawrence, 81 Prince street.
Hampson, Frederick, 461 Dean street.
Hampson, Mrs. Emma, 461 Dean street.

Hellwick, Dora, 191 Fulton street.
Hellwick, Emma, 191 Fulton street.

Jackson, George, 355 Hicks street.
Jennings, John W., 47 Concord street.

Keenan, John, Marcy avenue.
Kraft, Geo., Boerum st., near Bushwick ave.

Leek, Christopher, Marcy avenue.
Leyden, James, 199 State street.
Lidigate, Margaret, 1189 Atlantic avenue.
Lunt, Charles, 452 Hart street.
Lunt, Josephine, 452 Hart street.
Leverich, Caleb, 105 Clermont avenue.

McClair, 94 Hudson avenue.
McLellan, Edward, New Pearl street, N. Y.
McLellan, Mrs. Jane, New Pearl st., N. Y.
McLellan, James, New Pearl street, N. Y.
McLellan, Mary A., New Pearl st., N. Y.
McGuigan, James, New Pearl street, N. Y.
McCullough, John, 244 Pacific street.
McCullough, Donald Ross, 244 Pacific st.
McGinnis, —— 11 Adams street.
McGinnis, —— 11 Adams street.
McNeil, James, 160 Myrtle avenue.
Martin, Timothy, 37 Lawrence street.
Mulvadey, Mary, 11 Little Water street.
Merton, G. S., Galveston, Texas.
Montrose, Joseph F., Navy street.

Nathan, Stephen, 66 Prince street.

Pampool, Lena, 191 Fulton street.
Pollard, William, Flushing and Grand aves.

Reigler, Joseph, 296 Atlantic avenue.
Rothwell, Adelaide, 1,191 Atlantic avenue.
Rossel, —— (Cuban), 62 Fulton street.

Suntz, Henry, 289 Court street.
Suntz, Charles, 289 Court street.
Sorlemer, George, Pearl and Concord sts.
Stephens, George, 214 Jay street.
Stedall, A., 45 Flatbush avenue.
Steele, Daniel, 33 Ninth street.

Tracey, John, 277 Wyckoff street.
Turpinghi, William, 14th st. and Fifth ave.

Vables, —— (Cuban), 62 Fulton street.

Vecht, Christian, Smith street.

Wroe, Charles, 191 Prince street.
Wroe, Charles, Jr., 191 Prince street.

LATEST REPORT OF MISSING PERSONS.

Since the above list was prepared, the following persons have been reported to the police as yet missing:

Byrnes, Bernard, 17, 233 Plymouth street.

Francis, George, 30, New York.

Game, Robert, 20, 179 Butler street.
Gannon, John, 18, 81 Gold street, N. Y.
Gibbs, Mary, 45, Sullivan street.

Hayes, Samuel, 20, Fifth avenue.
Hesdra, Mary A., 25, 153 Gold street.
Hennessey, George, 29, 6 Duffield st.

Jennison, H., 19, Fourth ave., cor. Wyckoff street.
Jennison, A., 17, Fourth ave., cor. Wyckoff street.

Jordan, Fred., 19, 500 Pacific street.

Morgan, Frank, 20, 224 Atlantic avenue.

Page, Sarah A., 48, 153 Gold street.
Page, Addie S., 23, 153 Gold street.

Russell, Arthur, 23, 334 Atlantic avenue.

Smith, Mrs., 52, 141 Sands street.
Simpson, Mrs., 24, 141 Sands street.

West, Catharine, Hartford, Conn.
White, William, 20, Smith street.
Wayland, Maggie, ——
Warner, John, 27, 438 Atlantic avenue.

www.ingramcontent.com/pod-product-compliance
Lightning Source LLC
Chambersburg PA
CBHW032123080426
42733CB00008B/1035